Match the Word to the Number

one

two

three

four

five

six

3

1

5

2

6

4

Match the Word to the Number

seven

eight

nine

ten

eleven

twelve

9

12

11

7

10

8

Read the Numbers
Connect the Dots
Connect the dots in order
from 1 to 10

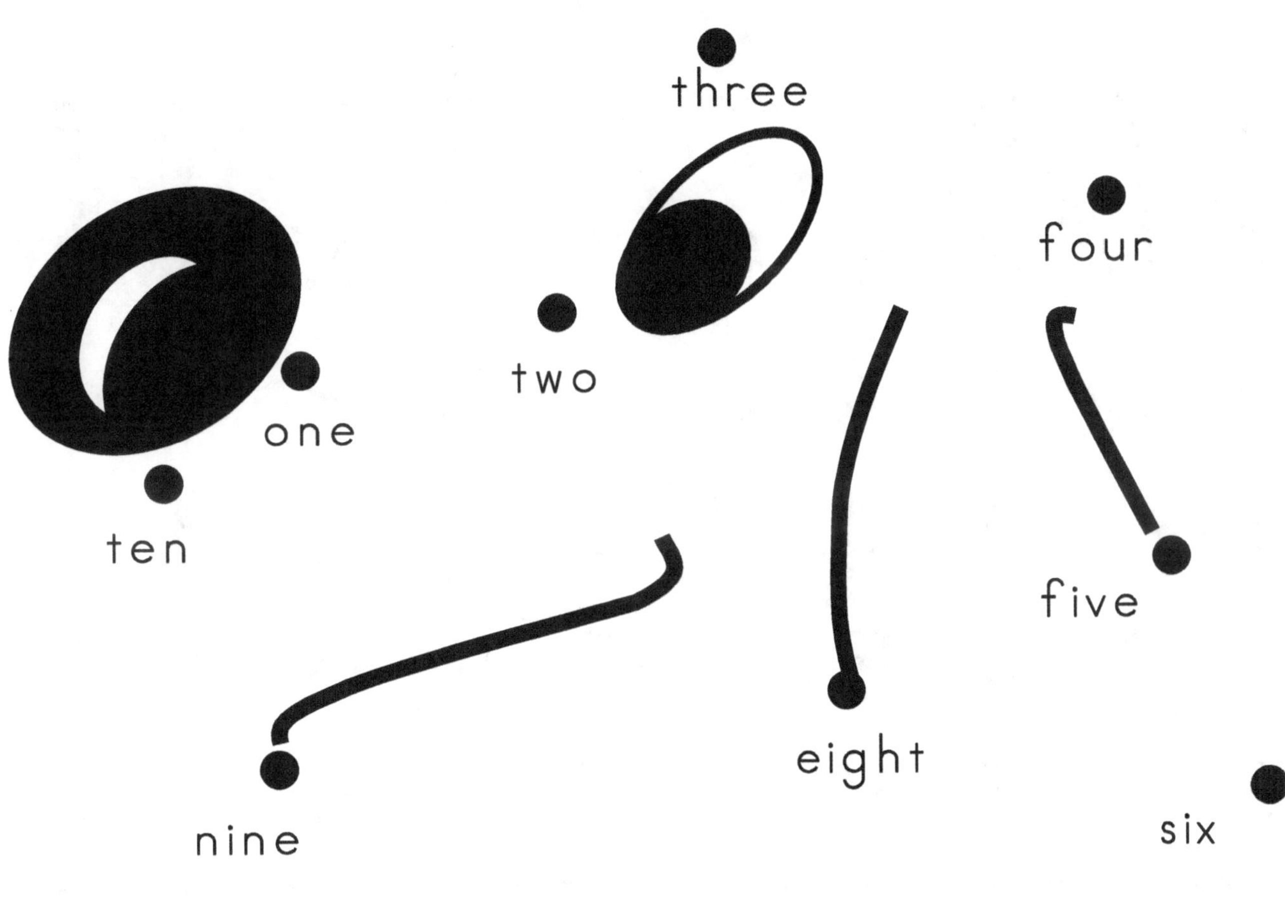

Word Search 1

Read each word and find it in the puzzle below.

A	E	Z	S	F	O	U	R	E	M
F	I	V	E	V	U	M	A	F	F
N	J	D	V	T	W	E	L	V	E
T	H	R	E	E	T	E	N	A	T
O	L	I	N	O	J	N	P	V	Y
S	C	A	C	N	E	I	G	H	T
T	W	O	R	E	F	N	S	I	X
E	L	E	V	E	N	E	E	F	A

one	two	three
four	five	six
seven	eight	nine
ten	eleven	twelve

Match the Color to the Object

red

orange

yellow

green

blue

purple

Match the Color to the Object

white

black

gray

pink

brown

gold

Read and Write the Words
For Animals that are Pets

Match the Picture to the Word

gerbil

bird

dog

cat

fish

Read and Write the Words
For Animals on the Farm

cow

cow

pig

pig

sheep

sheep

horse

horse

chicken

chicken

Match the Picture to the Word

sheep

horse

chicken

pig

cow

Read and Write the Words
For Animals on the Farm

Match the Picture to the Word

rabbit

turkey

duck

donkey

goat

Read and Trace the Sight Words

a   I have a ball.

I   I have a bat.

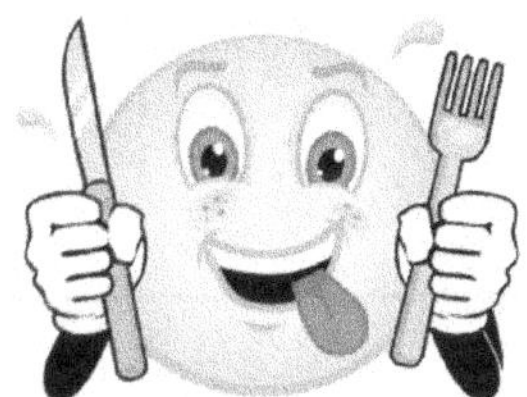

am   I am hungry.

an   I want an apple.

as   I sit as I eat.

Write the sentences with the correct words

a   I   am
an   as

___ ____ hungry.

___ sit ___ I eat.

___ want ___ apple.

___ have ___ bat.

Write your own sentences with the words

> a   I   a m
>
> a n   a s

Match the Word to the Picture

ball

bat

apple

dog

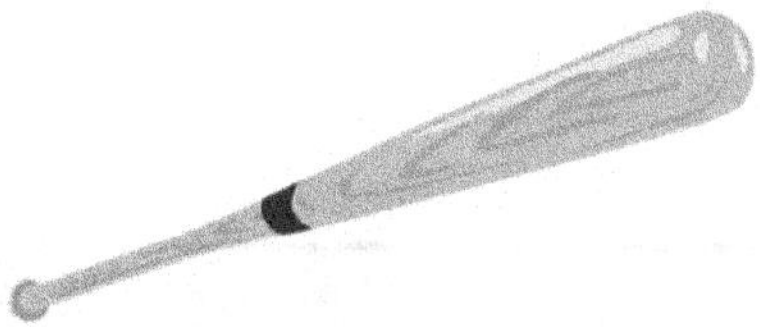

cat

happy

Read and Trace the Sight Words

at I am at school.

at   at   at

be   I will be happy. 

be   be   be

by   Sit by me.

by   by   by

do Do you like dogs? 

do   do   do

go I go to sleep. 

go   go   go

Write the sentences with the correct words

at   be   by
do   go

You can ____ it!

I sit ___ my desk.

I will ____ sad.

They ____ ____ bus.

18

Write your own sentences with the words

at   be   by

do   go

Word Search 2
Read each word and find it in the
puzzle below.

```
A P P L E E C N F U
K E X C T S B A T E
P E N N P O U C T A
S C H O O L F I G T
A S O C A T B A L L
D S I T E S L E E P
E U E H U N G R Y T
D O G H A P P Y Y V
```

bat	hungry	apple
eat	sit	ball
dog	cat	happy
sad	school	sleep

Read and Trace the Sight Words

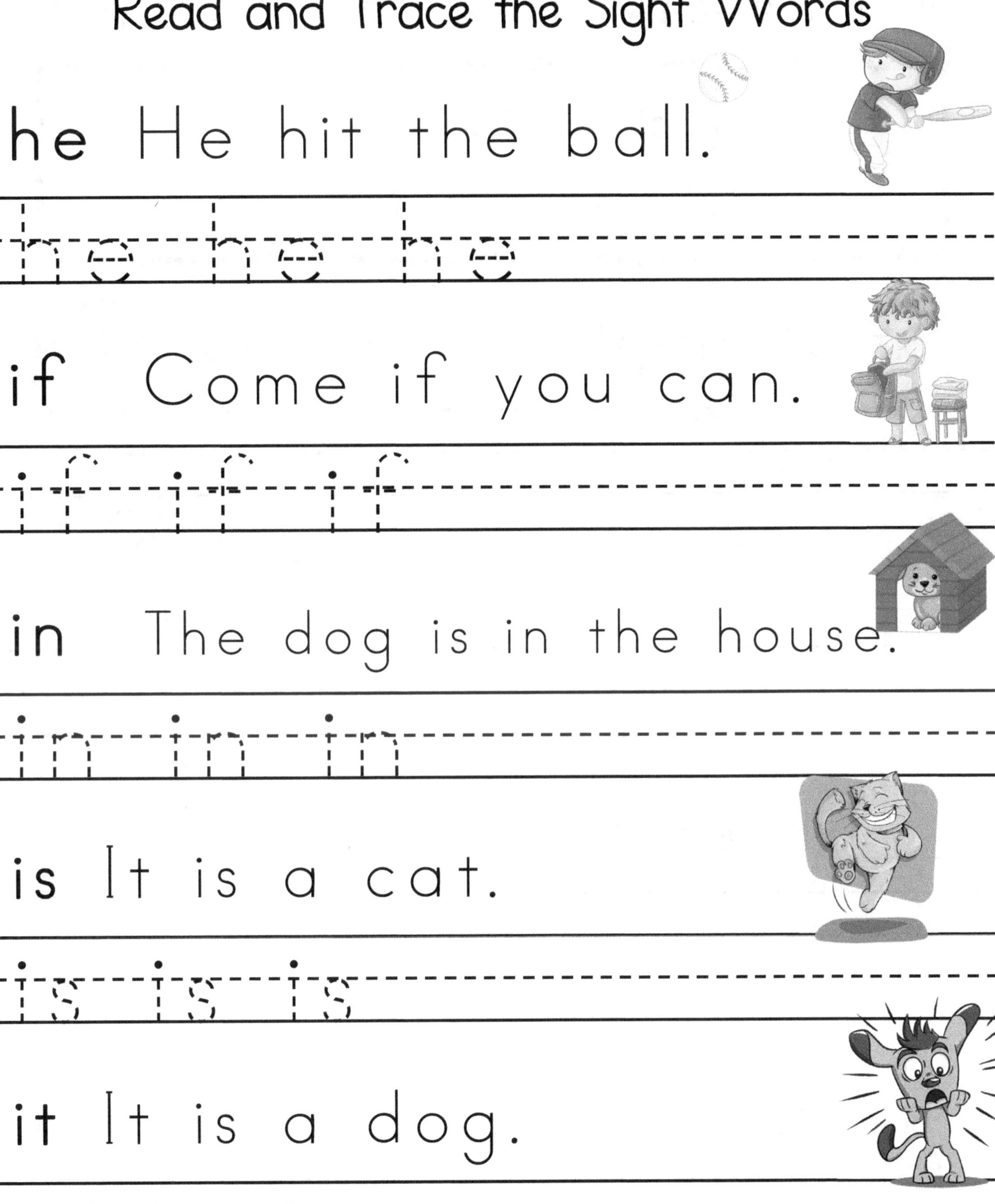

he He hit the ball.

if Come if you can.

in The dog is in the house.

is It is a cat.

it It is a dog.

Write the sentences with the correct words

> he   if   in
>
> is   it

Eat an apple ___ you want.

What is ___?

____ likes the kite.

The dog ____ ____ the tub.

Write your own sentences with the words

he   if   in

is   it

Follow the Sight Words Through the Maze

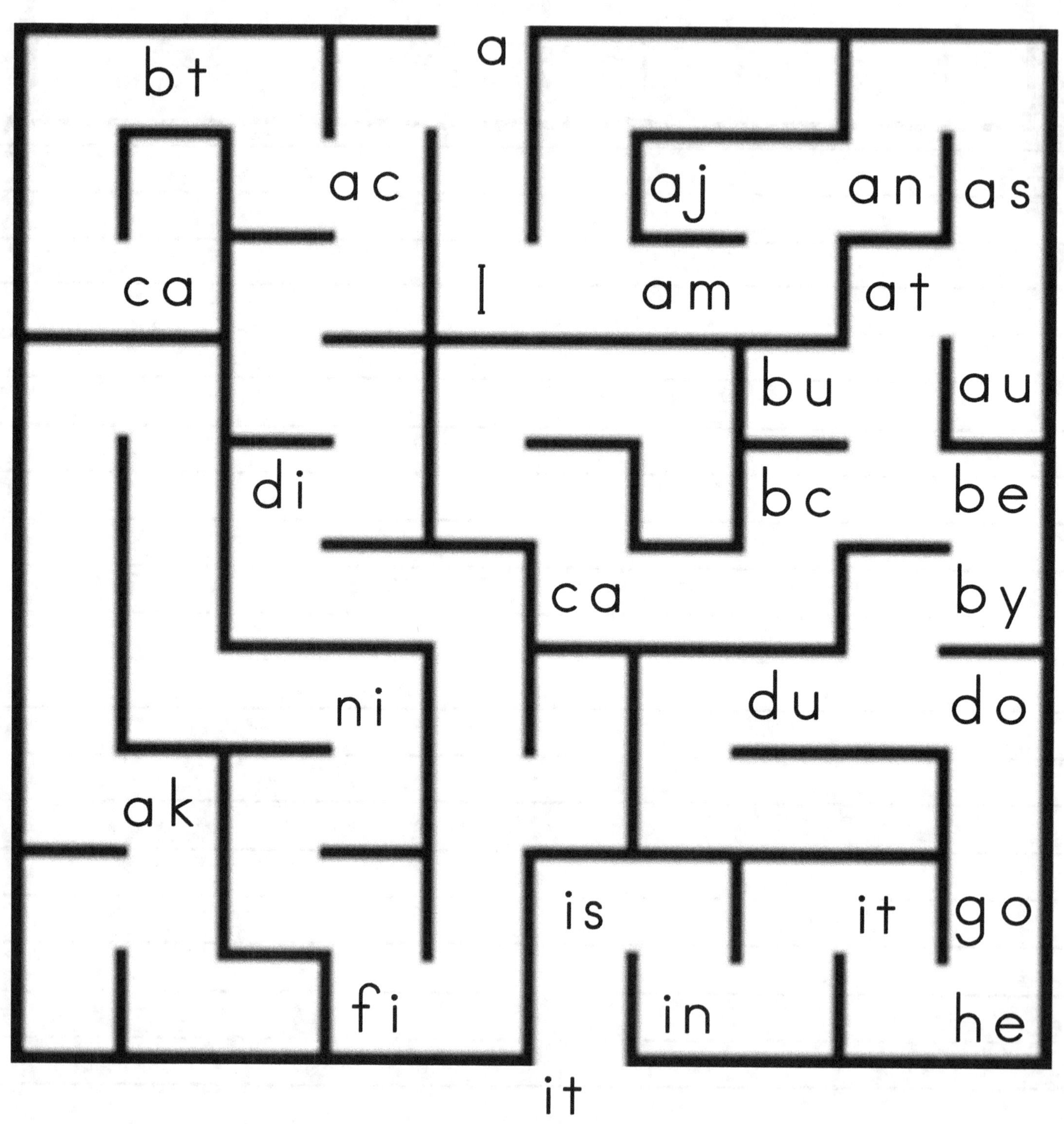

Read and Trace the Sight Words

my   This is my ball.

my my my

no   No, I can't go.

no no no

of   Get out of bed.

of of of of

on   Put the ball on top.

on on on on

or   Is it a cat or dog?

or or or or

Write the sentences with the correct words

> my   no   of
> on   or

Walk ahead ____ me.

There are ____ dogs here.

Here is ____ magic ball.

Is it ___ ____ off?

Write your own sentences with the words

my   no   of
on   or

Match the Word to the Picture

sit

sleep

school

desk

sad

bus

Read and Trace the Sight Words

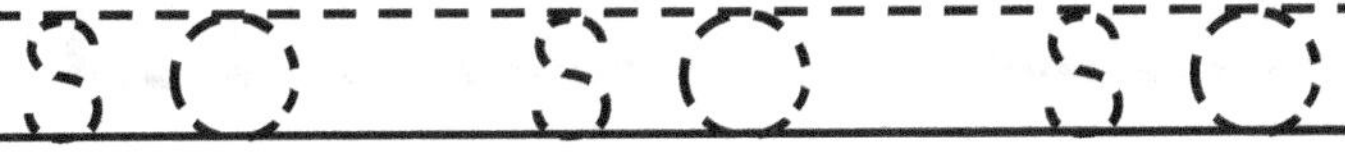

so You are so good.

so so so

to I walk to the bus. 

to to to

up Go up the hill. 

up up up

we We like math.

we we we

all We are all here. 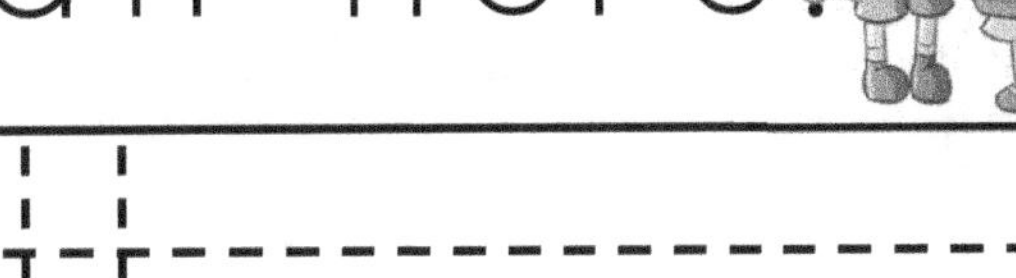

all all all

Write the sentences with the correct words

> so   to   up
> we   all

Giraffe are ___ tall.

___ go sledding.

They ___ went.

It went ___ ___ the moon.

Write your own sentences with the words

so   to   up
we   all

Word Search 3
Read each word and find it in the puzzle below.

```
Q  M  V  W  P  G  E  T  K  V
L  G  M  A  G  I  C  B  I  H
S  E  U  N  S  O  A  I  T  O
C  P  I  T  Y  I  C  E  E  U
U  K  W  T  C  O  M  E  L  S
P  U  T  U  W  H  A  T  L  E
D  U  R  B  W  W  A  L  K  J
N  E  F  P  T  O  P  B  E  D
```

come	house	kite
want	tub	what
get	bed	top
put	walk	magic

Read and Trace the Sight Words

and I have a ball and bat.

and and and

are They are here.

are are are

but I want to go, but I can't.

but but but

can Can you go?

can can can

day Have a good day.

day day day

Write the sentences with the correct words

> and   are   but
> can   day

Dolphins ____ jumping.

Have a great ___!

I like eggs ___ bacon.

I ___ help, ___ not now.

Write your own sentences with the words

and   are   but

can   day

Follow the Sight Words Through the Maze

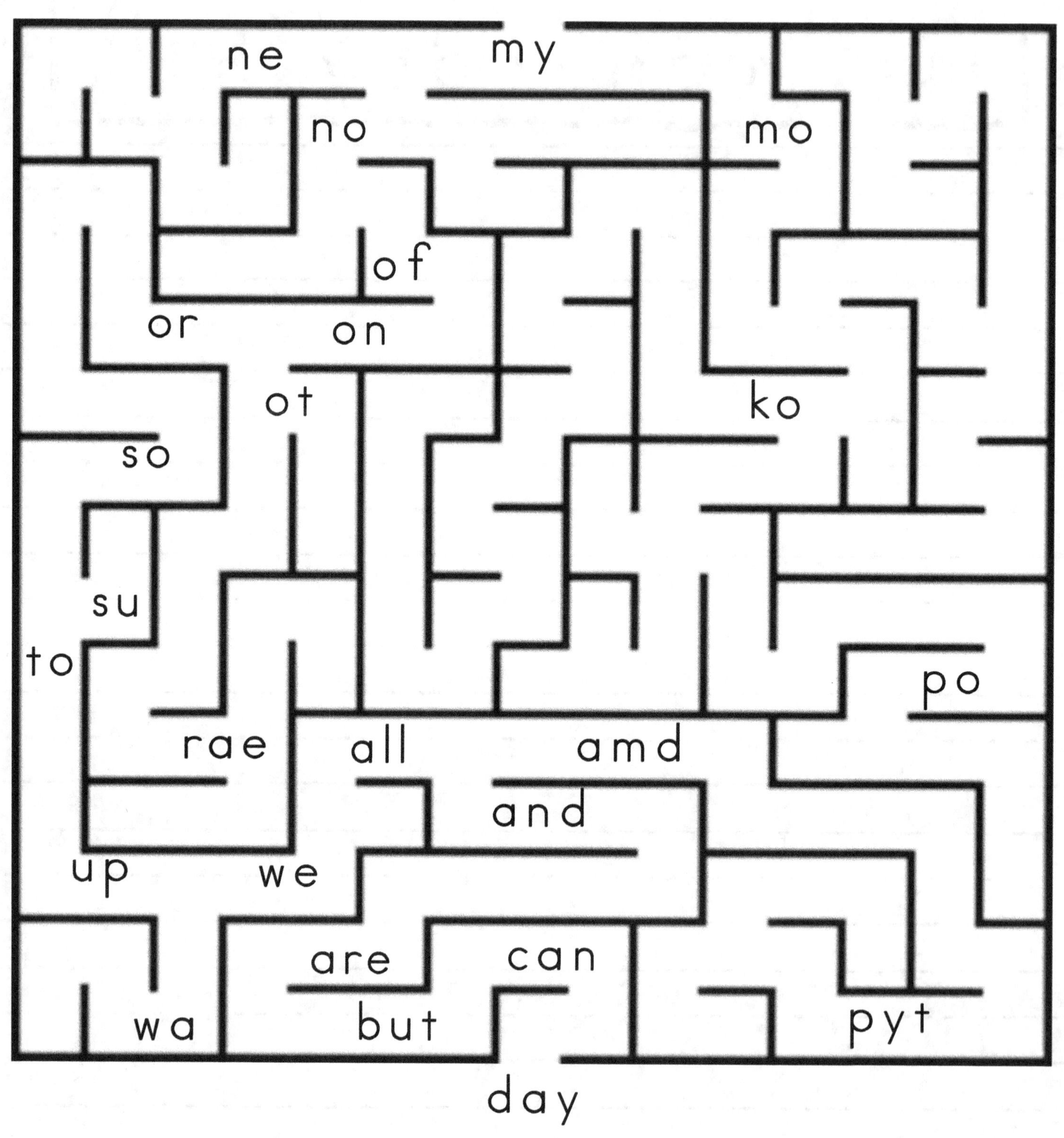

Read and Trace the Sight Words

did Did the cat eat?

did did did

for It's time for bed.

for for for

get I will get a fish.

get get get

had She had a snack.

had had had

has He has a book.

has has has

Write the sentences with the correct words

> **did   for   get**
> **had   has**

He ___ a yellow ball. 

She made a cake _____ me. 

I ___ to stay in bed. 

___ you ___ the food? 

Write your own sentences with the words

did for get
had has

Match the Word to the Picture

math

hill

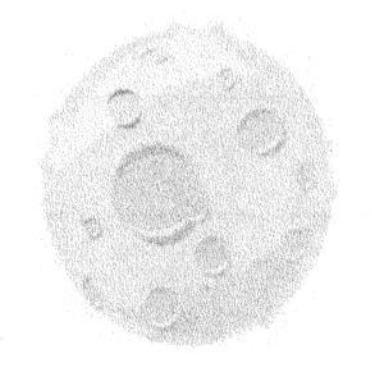

cake

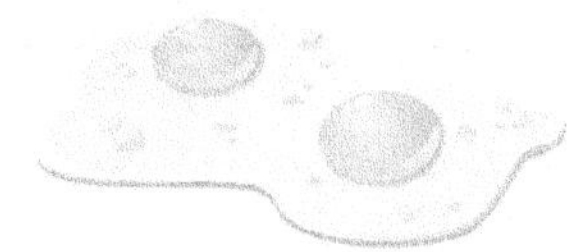

sled

moon

eggs

Read and Trace the Sight Words

her Give it to her.

her her her

him I saw him.

him him him

his This is his dog.

his his his

how How do you read.

how how how

its The dog is in its house.

its its its

Write the sentences with the correct words

> her   him   his
> how   its

The water balloon hit ____.

She sat at ____ desk.

The dog took ____ bath.

____ was ____ magic show?

Write your own sentences with the words

her   him   his
how   its

Word Search 4
Read each word and find it in the puzzle below.

```
N  F  Y  E  B  A  S  H  D  C  Z
O  B  E  R  A  P  T  E  V  A  Q
W  C  I  T  C  D  H  D  E  Q  G
A  N  E  E  O  A  E  A  F  Y  O
I  Z  R  A  N  Y  L  P  I  E  O
S  N  A  C  K  Y  P  H  S  L  D
J  U  M  P  C  A  K  E  H  L  M
K  O  E  R  S  L  I  K  E  O  K
D  O  L  P  H  I  N  M  F  W  Z
```

good	day	bacon
jump	dolphin	help
now	like	snack
fish	yellow	cake

Read and Trace the Sight Words

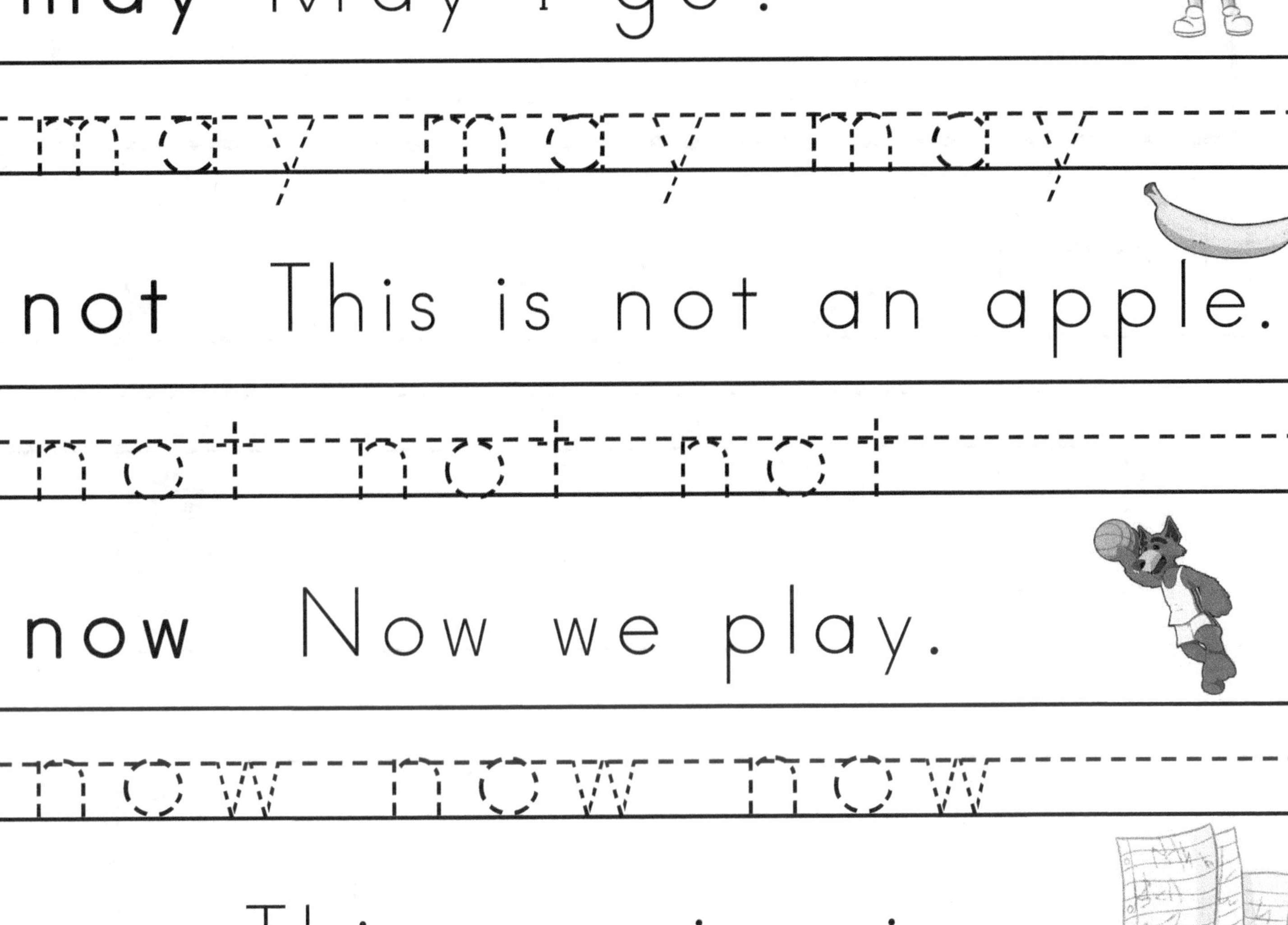

may May I go?

may may may

not This is not an apple.

not not not

now Now we play.

now now now

one This one is mine.

one one one

out The frog came out.

out out out

Write the sentences with the correct words

may   not   now
one   out

That is ___ a dog.

I have ____ apple.

____ I have some food?

___ he will go ___.

Write your own sentences with the words

may not now

one out

Unscramble the Sight Words

idd   ----------------

rof   ----------------

teg   ----------------

ahd   ----------------

sha   ----------------

aym   ----------------

onw   ----------------

tou   ----------------

reh   ----------------

hmi   ----------------

ayd   ----------------

anc   ----------------

sti   ----------------

ont   ----------------

eno   ----------------

nad   ----------------

Read and Trace the Sight Words

see I see a bear.

see see see

she She likes candy. 

she she she

the Please sit by me. 

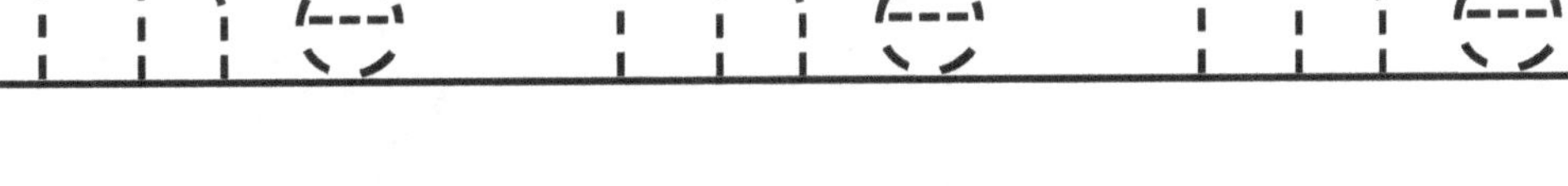

two I have two cookies. 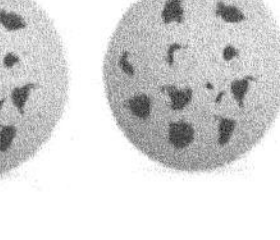

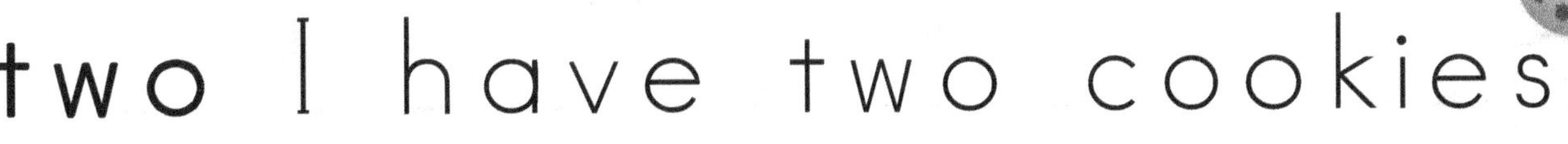

use I use my pen. 

use use use

Write the sentences with the correct words

see   she   the

two   use

___ is in school.

___ bee is flying.

I ___ my umbrella.

Do you ___ the ___ birds?

Write your own sentences with the words

see she the
two use

51

Match the Word to the Picture

house

bath

frog

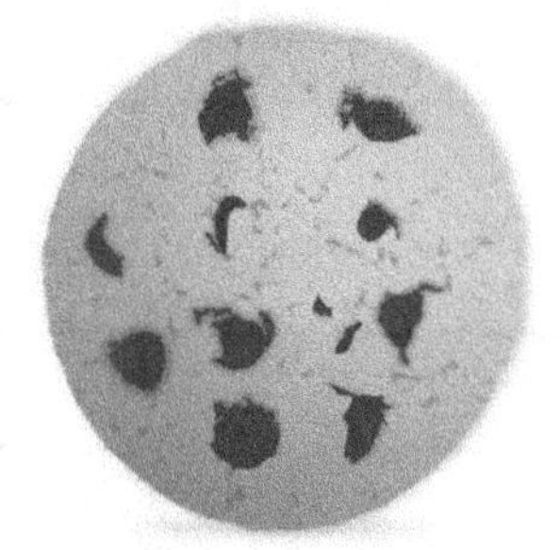

food

cookie

bear

Read and Trace the Sight Words

was He was fast.

was was was

way This is the way.

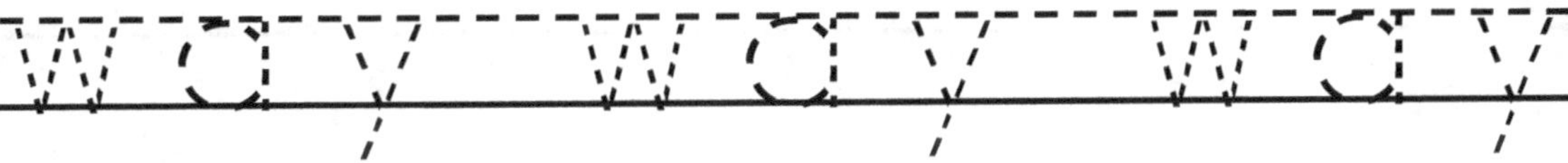

way way way

who Who is this?

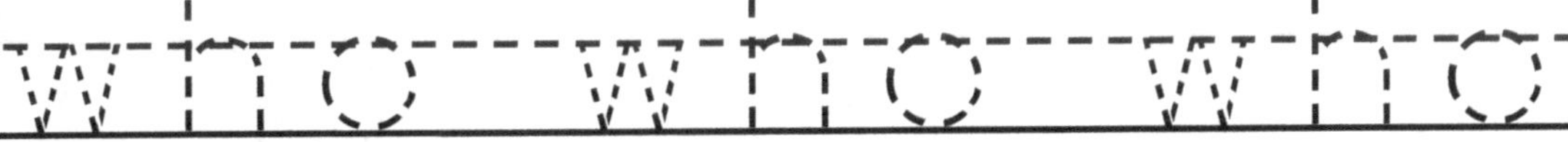

who who who

you Do you like dogs?

you you you

been I have been sick.

been been been

was way who
you been

I have ___ busy.

Do ___ have a book?

___ is flying?

____ this the ____ out?

Write your own sentences with the words

was   way   who
you   been

Word Search 5
Read each word and find it in the
puzzle below.

```
U  E  E  F  F  M  L  I  C  X  I
N  F  E  E  B  I  N  W  A  Q  P
E  F  R  O  G  N  I  F  N  E  M
F  Q  H  X  A  E  P  A  D  L  I
L  S  O  M  E  V  L  S  Y  G  B
Y  F  O  O  D  O  E  T  U  K  E
I  P  D  P  N  I  A  P  E  N  A
N  A  E  I  A  G  S  I  C  K  R
G  U  J  E  O  O  O  E  B  I  R  D
```

mine	frog	food
some	bear	candy
please	pen	flying
bird	fast	sick

Read and Trace the Sight Words

come Come over here.

come come come

down The tree fell down.

down down down

each We each got one.

each each each

find Did you find it?

find find find

from He jumped from it.

from from from

Write the sentences with the correct words

come   down   each
find   from

We walk ____ here.

We ____ got one.

Can you ____ the fish?

____ ____ the stairs.

Write your own sentences with the words

come down each
find from

Unscramble the Sight Words

dnwo _______________

caeh _______________

dfni _______________

asw _______________

orfm _______________

ouy _______________

lal _______________

woh _______________

ecmo _______________

nebe _______________

ayw _______________

seu _______________

owt _______________

teh _______________

ehs _______________

ese _______________

Read and Trace the Sight Words

Write the sentences with the correct words

have   into   like
long   look

They went ___ the boat.

Do you ___ an eraser?

It went for a ___ walk.

I ___ to ___ at books.

Write your own sentences with the words

have   into   like
long   look

Match the Word to the Picture

book

candy

pen

boat

bird

umbrella

Read and Trace the Sight Words

made I made pizza.

made made

make Make a square.

make make

many Many animals live here.

many many

more Can I play more?

more more

part It's missing a part.

part part

made   make   many
more   part

Can I have ____ of that?

I have ____ shells.

He ____ a pizza.

Can you ____ ____?

Write your own sentences with the words

made   make   many
more   part

Word Search 6
Read each word and find it in the
puzzle below.

W	Z	A	A	I	L	C	G	M	K
I	Q	H	M	P	I	Z	Z	A	W
W	A	L	K	I	F	P	C	E	A
H	E	G	F	E	L	L	N	U	Y
D	O	W	N	B	O	A	T	W	S
T	P	L	A	Y	T	R	E	E	M
F	I	N	D	T	O	Y	O	N	L
S	T	A	I	R	S	B	E	T	N

find	tree	fell
down	walk	stairs
toy	way	went
boat	pizza	play

Read and Trace the Sight Words

said He said, "Let's go!"

said said said

some We ate some pie.

some some some

than I like dogs more than cats.

than than than

that What is that?

that that that

them We went to see them.

them them them

Write the sentences with the correct words

> said   some   than
> that   them

The rabbit is faster ____ the turtle.

What is ____ sound? 

I ____, "good-bye." 

____ of ____ played.

Write your own sentences with the words

said   some   than
that   them

Unscramble the Sight Words

aehv ______________   emor ______________

toni ______________   tapr ______________

eikl ______________   disa ______________

gonl ______________   emso ______________

kolo ______________   hant ______________

edma ______________   taht ______________

aemk ______________   ehmt ______________

ynmn ______________   ownd ______________

Read and Trace the Sight Words

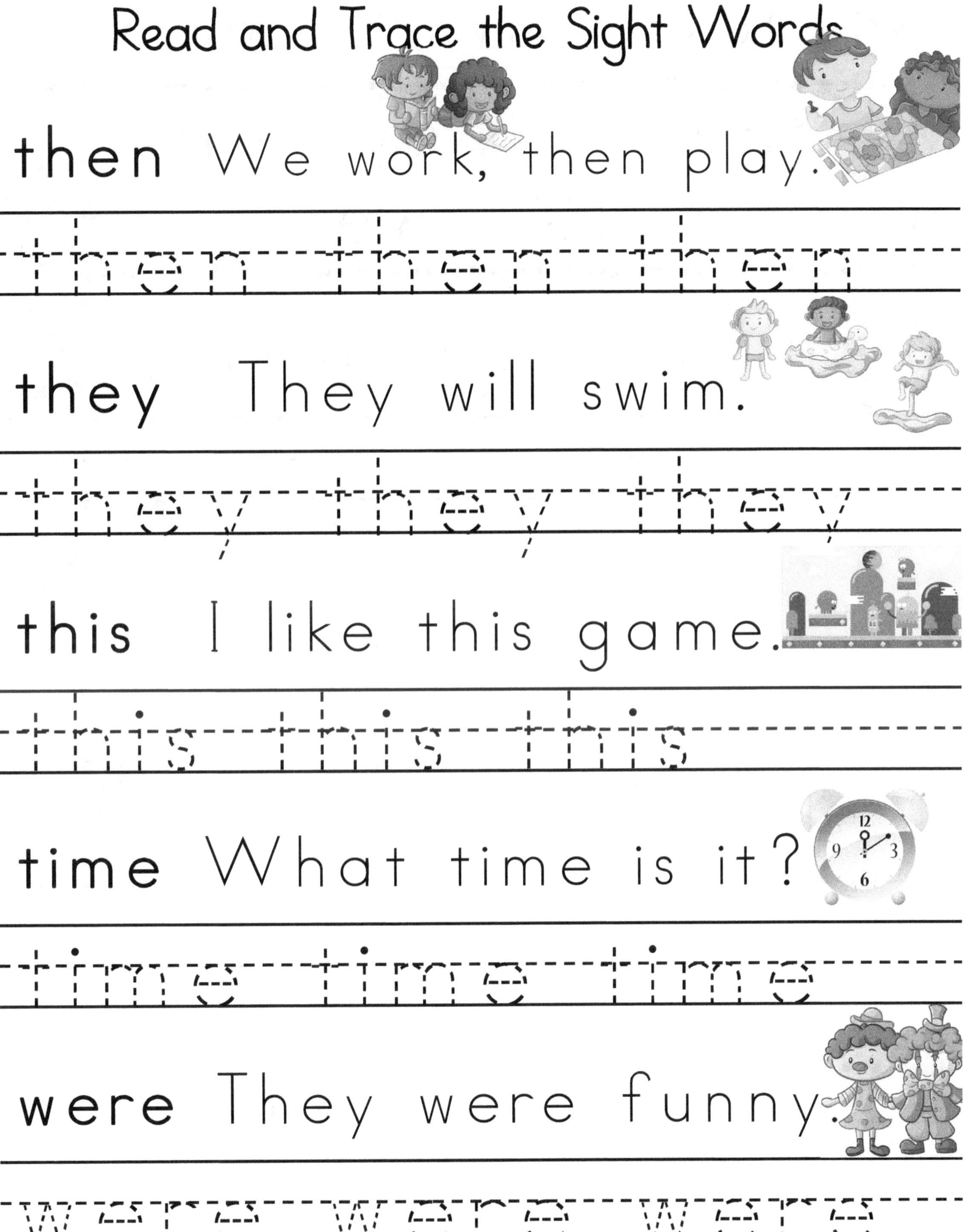

then   We work, then play.

then then then

they   They will swim.

they they they

this   I like this game.

this this this

time   What time is it?

time time time

were   They were funny.

were were were

Write the sentences with the correct words

| then | they | this |
| time | were | |

It's time to go to class.

_____ is the best game.

I wish I _____ an astronaut.

_____ worked, _____ played.

Write your own sentences with the words

then they this
time were

Write your own sentences with the words

Match the Word to the Picture

pizza

square

shell

pie

rabbit

turtle

Read and Trace the Sight Words

what What food is good?

what what

when When does break start?

when when

will Will you help?

will will

with I'll go with you.

with with

your What's your name?

your your

what   when   will
with   your

Can I use ____ pencil?

He went ____ her.

____ time is it?

____ ____ you go?

Write your own sentences with the words

what   when   will
    with   your

Word Search 7

Read each word and find it in the puzzle below.

M	C	N	A	M	E	X	B	I	P	P
E	W	G	E	F	S	M	E	C	L	B
R	S	X	E	A	Q	R	S	L	A	R
A	W	O	R	K	E	O	T	A	M	E
B	S	O	U	N	D	B	T	S	O	A
B	T	U	R	T	L	E	Z	S	H	K
I	G	A	M	E	F	U	N	N	Y	C
T	V	M	S	T	A	R	T	I	I	M
I	H	C	N	I	I	S	W	I	M	I

rabbit	turtle	sound
work	swim	game
funny	class	best
break	start	name

Read and Trace the Sight Words

about I learned about fish.

about about

could I could do it.

could could

first I was in first place.

first first

other Help each other.

other other

their We went to their house.

their their

Write the sentences with the correct words

about   could   first
other   their

They were own ____ way.

He talked _____ his trip.

When can we see each ____?

I _____ get _____ place.

Write your own sentences with the words

about could first
other their

Unscramble the Sight Words

rehti -----------------   lilw -----------------

vahe -----------------   henw -----------------

rehot -----------------   twah -----------------

ifsrt -----------------   eerw -----------------

cdlou -----------------   emti -----------------

tbauo -----------------   sith -----------------

royu -----------------   yeth -----------------

hitw -----------------   nteh -----------------

Read and Trace the Sight Words

there   There is a ball.

these   These are my books.

water   Fish are in the water.

which   Which house is yours?

words   She reads many words.

Write the sentences with the correct words

> there   these   water
> which   words

________ scissors cut well.

________ bag is yours?

He knows many ____.

________ are many fish in the ______.

Write your own sentences with the words

there these water
which words

Match the Word to the Picture

pencil

time

fish

water

bag

letter

Read and Trace the Sight Words

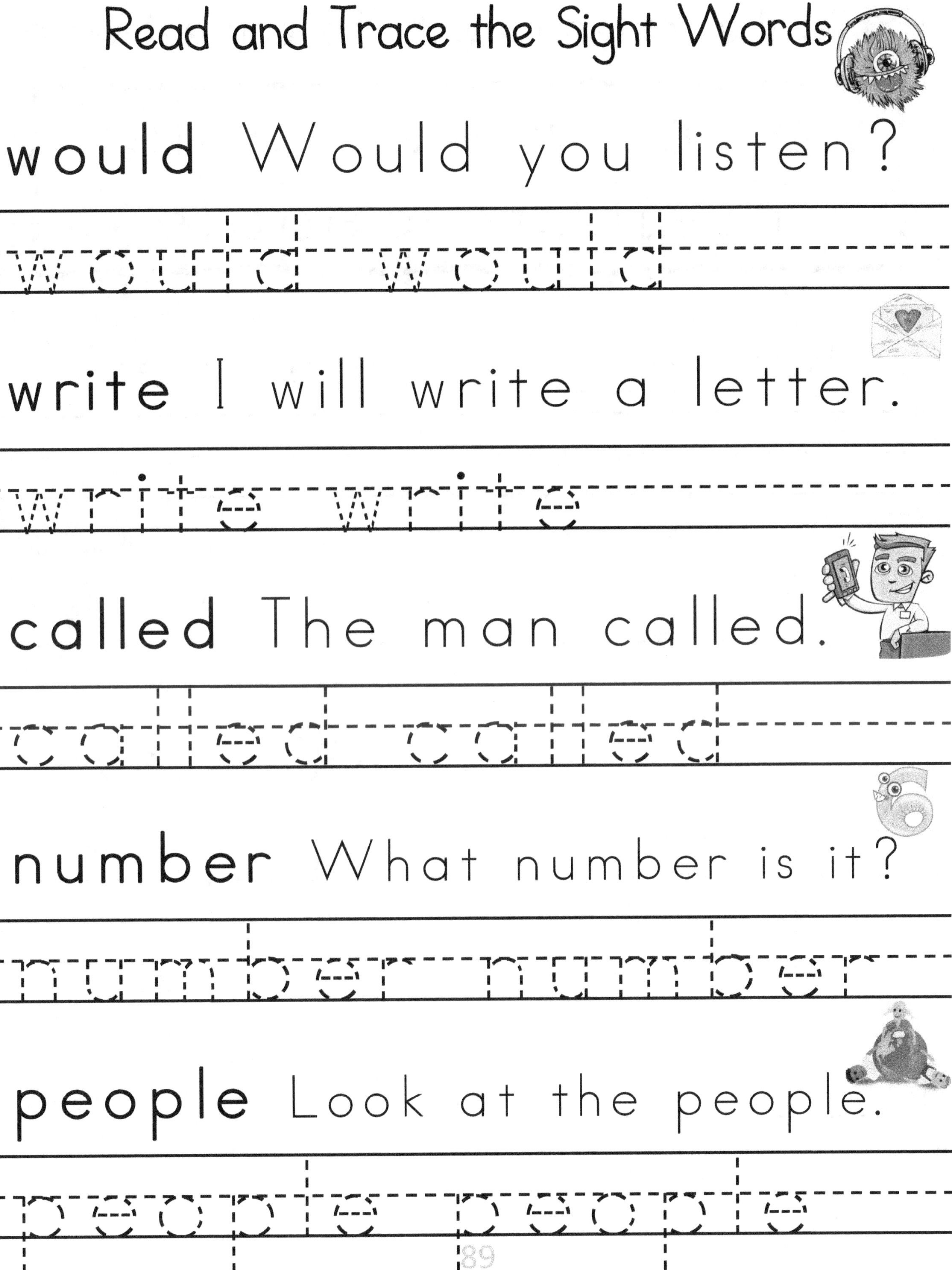

would Would you listen?

would would

write I will write a letter.

write write

called The man called.

called called

number What number is it?

number number

people Look at the people.

people people

Write the sentences with the correct words

> would write called
> number people

What _______ comes next?

Many _______ live here.

Wait until _______ .

I ____ ____ a letter.

would write called
number people

Word Search 8
Read each word and find it in the
puzzle below.

```
M  W  H  E  R  E  R  V  S  A  Y
S  L  I  S  T  E  N  J  M  K  A
C  U  U  I  I  L  E  A  R  N  H
I  W  I  D  R  E  A  D  E  O  E
S  A  M  O  P  E  A  C  H  W  L
S  T  I  V  S  C  K  K  F  E  P
O  E  A  N  D  L  E  T  T  E  R
R  R  P  L  A  C  E  T  A  L  K
S  X  A  O  A  S  Y  E  V  A  Y
```

learn	place	help
talk	where	each
read	water	scissors
know	listen	letter

Unscramble the Sight Words

eerht

eehst

reawt

chwih

sorwd

duolw

trwie

omrf

eimt

eerw

eeoppl

alclde

erumnb

Match the Word to the Picture

people

first

number

down

time

called

Word Search 9
Read each word and find it in the puzzle below.

```
H  K  G  A  A  U  O  O  U  C  U  J
I  O  O  F  Y  S  Q  F  U  N  N  Y
L  I  T  T  L  E  G  R  U  H  F  O
Y  E  L  L  O  W  B  L  U  E  V  G
M  S  R  W  H  E  R  E  R  R  A  R
P  D  E  G  J  U  M  P  D  E  Y  E
L  R  D  H  E  L  P  U  R  P  L  E
A  W  A  Y  H  E  R  E  B  A  T  N
Y  A  T  R  R  F  O  R  A  N  G  E
H  V  U  C  O  N  B  T  M  N  T  I
```

away	green	blue
here	funny	help
here	jump	little
red	yellow	where
purple	play	orange

Word Search 1
Read each word and find it in the
puzzle below.

one   two   three
four   five   six
seven   eight   nine
ten   eleven   twelve

Word Search 2
Read each word and find it in the
puzzle below.

bat   hungry   apple
eat   sit   ball
dog   cat   happy
sad   school   sleep

Follow the Sight Words Through the Maze

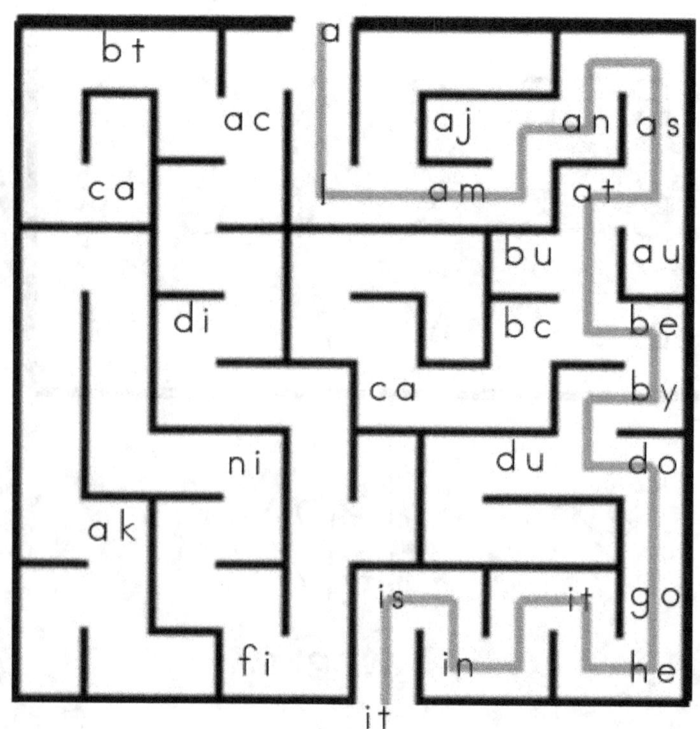

Word Search 3
Read each word and find it in the
puzzle below.

come   house   kite
want   tub   what
get   bed   top
put   walk   magic

Follow the Sight Words Through the Maze

36

Word Search 4
Read each word and find it in the
puzzle below.

good   day   bacon
jump   dolphin   help
now   like   snack
fish   yellow   cake

44

Word Search 5
Read each word and find it in the
puzzle below.

mine   frog   food
some   bear   candy
please   pen   flying
bird   fast   sick

56

Word Search 6
Read each word and find it in the
puzzle below.

find   tree   fell
down   walk   stairs
toy   way   went
boat   pizza   play

68

Word Search 7
Read each word and find it in the
puzzle below.

M	C	N	A	M	E	X	B	I	P	P
E	W	G	E	F	S	M	E	C	L	B
R	S	X	E	A	Q	R	S	L	A	R
A	W	O	R	K	E	O	T	A	M	E
B	S	O	U	N	D	B	T	S	O	A
B	T	U	R	T	L	E	Z	S	H	K
I	G	A	M	E	F	U	N	N	Y	C
T	V	M	S	T	A	R	T	I	I	M
I	H	C	N	I	I	S	W	I	M	I

rabbit   turtle   sound
work   swim   game
funny   class   best
break   start   name

Word Search 8
Read each word and find it in the
puzzle below.

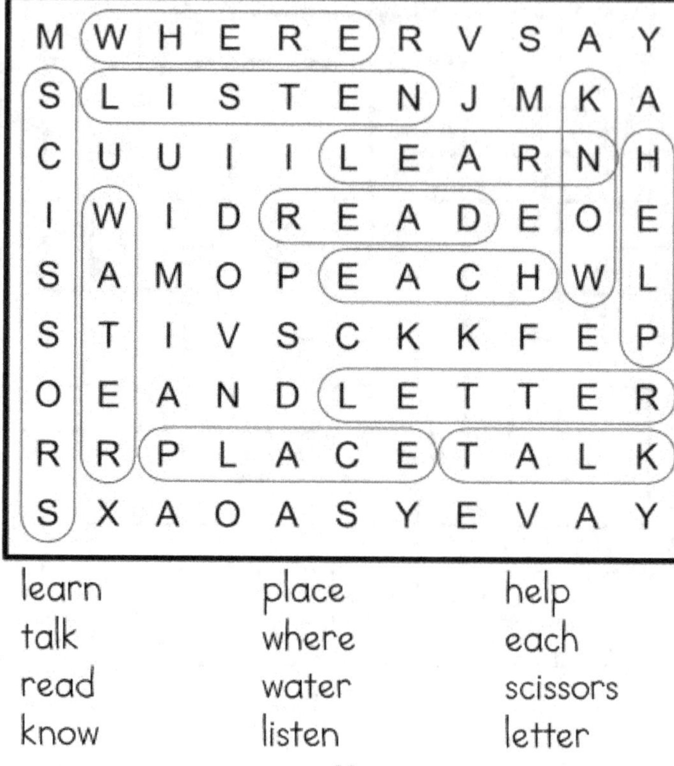

M	W	H	E	R	E	R	V	S	A	Y
S	L	I	S	T	E	N	J	M	K	A
C	U	U	I	I	L	E	A	R	N	H
I	W	I	D	R	E	A	D	E	O	E
S	A	M	O	P	E	A	C	H	W	L
S	T	I	V	S	C	K	K	F	E	P
O	E	A	N	D	L	E	T	T	E	R
R	R	P	L	A	C	E	T	A	L	K
S	X	A	O	A	S	Y	E	V	A	Y

learn   place   help
talk   where   each
read   water   scissors
know   listen   letter

Word Search 9
Read each word and find it in the
puzzle below.

H	K	G	A	A	U	O	O	U	C	U	J
I	O	O	F	Y	S	Q	F	U	N	N	Y
L	I	T	T	L	E	G	R	U	H	F	O
Y	E	L	L	O	W	B	L	U	E	V	G
M	S	R	W	H	E	R	E	R	R	A	R
P	D	E	G	J	U	M	P	D	E	Y	E
L	R	D	H	E	L	P	U	R	P	L	E
A	W	A	Y	H	E	R	E	B	A	T	N
Y	A	T	R	R	F	O	R	A	N	G	E
H	V	U	C	O	N	B	T	M	N	T	I

away   green   blue
here   funny   help
here   jump   little
red   yellow   where
purple   play   orange